ONE WOMAN'S POETRY

ONE WOMAN'S POETRY

PAT HART BRUNSTRÖM

Copyright © 2015 Pat Hart Brunström
All rights reserved.

ISBN: 1514384329
ISBN 13: 9781514384329
Library of Congress Control Number: 2015909870
CreateSpace Independent Publishing Platform
North Charleston, South Carolina

For my family,
With love

CONTENTS

Tower Block · 1
The Murderer · 3
I Am A Girl · 4
With Love · 7
Safe House · 9
1986 · 11
Yellow Rape · 13
Good Friday · 15
In Dreams I Walk The Hills Again · 17
Bequests · 19
Antonio · 21
The Pool · 23
Prey · 25
Captain · 27
Menopause · 29
Starving · 31
The Apple · 33
The Arts Centre · 35
Pruning · 37
Free Love · 39
Canvasses · 41
Hungerford · 43
El Fuerte · 45

The Maggot	46
The Heron	49
The Present	51
Moseley Church	53
Friend You Must Talk	55
November	57
Conch	59
City Park	61
Quaking	63
Out Of Reach	65
Lost	67
Margaret	69
Riches	71
Silence	73
Looking At Shakespeare's Tomb And Thinking About Poor Yorick	75
For Conrad (The Betjeman Years)	77
Forty Years On	79
Sea Change	81
The Harvest	83
Killing	84
Poems	87
Fat Cat	89
This One	90
House Of The Binns	93
The Village	95
Love Poem To A Grandson	97
The Blizzard	99
The Valley	101
Back Off Life	103
Coming Home	105
Prawns	107
The Child	109
Costa Belloc	111

The 'Real World'	113
Loss	115
Conversation Piece	117
Lost And Found	119
Lifetimes	121
Paralysis	123
The Grub	125
Suburban Lady	127
Spillikins	129
Dog Days	131
English Heat Wave	133
Micro Madness	135
Guilt	137
On The Common	139
Yorkshire Sky	141
The Rose	143
While You Can	145
In Leatherworkers Street	147
Almost Dark	149
Model	151
Affluence	153
Andalucian Haiku	155
Summer Friends	157

Message from Pat

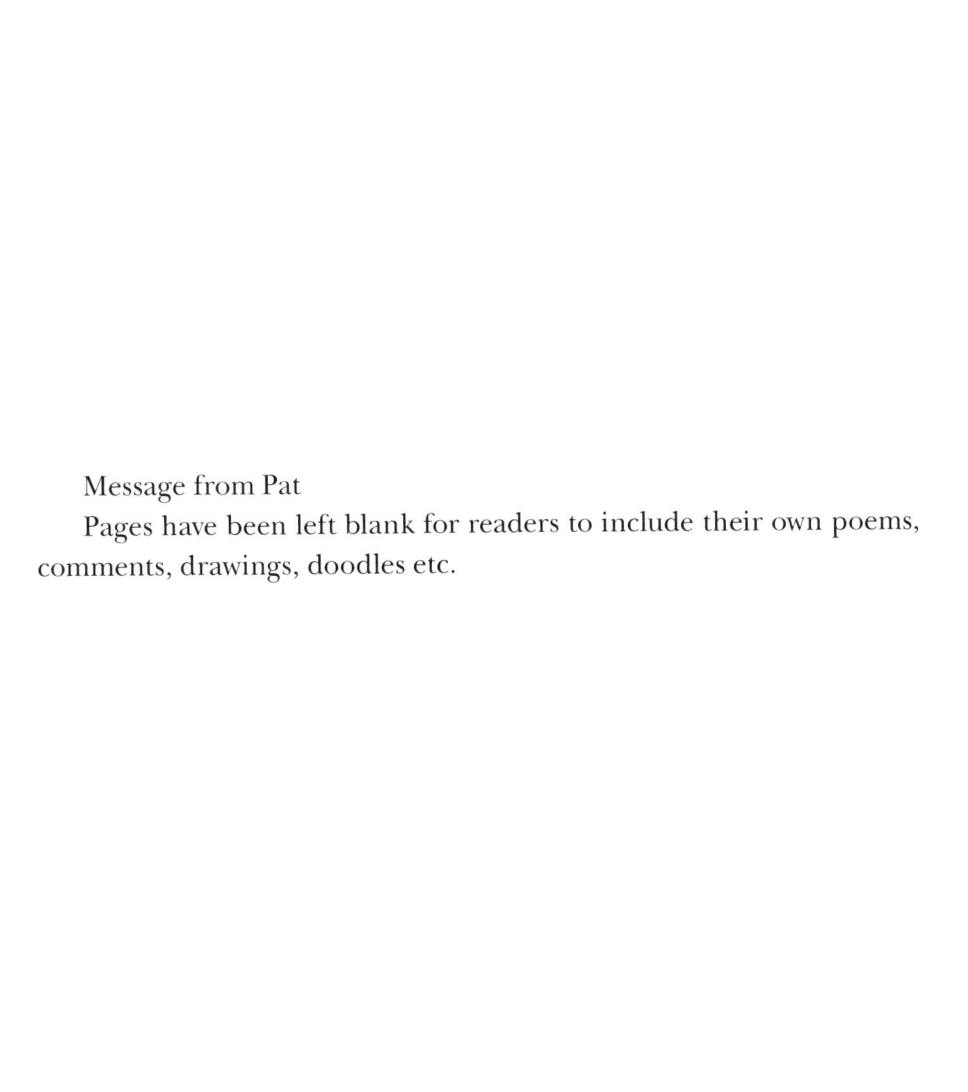

Pages have been left blank for readers to include their own poems, comments, drawings, doodles etc.

TOWER BLOCK

Let down your hair and weep, Rapunzel
as you sit at the window of your
tower block's thirteenth floor
in the core of the city.

Weep for your prince who will never come
to claim you and frame you in white lace
for the wedding of your dreams and schemes.

You must stay, Rapunzel, locked in your
isolated cell with no-one to tell
of your despair.

You must fight your dragon alone
in the stone cold dreariness
the bone deep weariness.

(The prince is elsewhere
with his horse on a course
to nowhereland.)
                      So let down your hair and scream.

THE MURDERER

The murderer strolls beneath the trees
His arm round his beloved
Pushing the thought of the other one
That other mother one
Far to the back
Of his dead
Mind

She restlessly stirs beneath his touch
Of guilt-weight her beloved
Pushing the thought of the other one
That other discovered one
Far to the back
Of her racked
Mind

I AM A GIRL

I am a girl.
I do not know how women feel
Except that they feel
Deeper - Truer - Surer - Stronger -
Than anything a girl may feel.

When I pass puberty
Then I will be a woman
And I will know.

A year ago it came
A mess upon the sheet
A problem to be dealt with
Monthly - The fount - In spate -
My breasts are swollen tender
My hips hollow with welcome
I feel raw to the touch -
A girl.

I will lose the prize - my maidenhead
Then I will be a woman
And I will know.
A year ago he came
In fumbling awkwardness
A stumbling accomplishment
Dual - Creation - Satiation -
I learn the round of love
The giddy tramplings of the male
I am a sightless Sybarite -
A girl.

When the ovaries kindle and the womb swells
When these breasts gush milk
Then I will be a woman
And I will know.

Some years ago they came
Fragile seed-humans spawned
Into an unknown future
Half fledged - Ecstatic - Usurpers -

They grow from my diminishing
Their debility nourishes my guilt
Their craving for certitude feeds my doubts
I am a girl.

When they are grown from me
Can stand alone
Then I will be a woman
And I will know.

Some years ago they left
Reciprocating all
Self sustainers leaving me free
I seek - Myself - once more -
Clutch at time fast running out
Thrust key on key into the deadlock
Lift layer from layer and find the core -
A girl.

When the cyclical slavery ceases
Then I will be a woman
And I will know.

A year ago it ceased
The brief metamorphosis
Leavening me erratic
Unphased - Floundering - Recast -
The womb shrinks and the memory drifts
Self doubt seeps into my blood
Thought beyond thought the face flushes
I am a girl.

When I am the ultimate
The last generation
Then I will be a woman
And I will know.

A year ago she died
A skeletal leaf blown
Silent towards the future
Leaving - Behind - Her child.

I am a girl.

WITH LOVE

For all the things I never did
And won't do now,
I do not care
For I can share
These hours with you.

For all the places never seen
And can't see now
I have the dream
Of where we've been
To walk with you

It's turned to this, our 'golden' youth,
The search for truth.
These deeds, this chase
In this time, in this place
We have this now.

SAFE HOUSE

They want us to live in fear.
The cosy home is a trap.
The box is a box that has boxed us up;
The box inside says "Bed down here.
It's comfy in our warm trap
So lifelong lifelong do it up
Don't demand, don't question – just fear."

1986

A fretful wind explores the indifferent streets,
shifts litter on the scummed flagstones,
but fails to move the crushed green glass
on which the coiled child rocks and moans
nuzzling his paper bag of dreams.

Re-counting coins the old man stumbles past,
aching to reach the pub and gain
his corner with the glass unspilt,
let warmth uncoil the bones and brain
and watch the coloured box of dreams.

A sparing sip and then the drink is nursed.
The pool of liquid, brown as bogs
recalls his youth, reflects his pain.
"Why did you send me here?" he rocks
and keens and grumbles at the dead.

"You should have kept me home, that was my place."
Blind to the farce he sips his drink
in rhythm with the boy who gropes
and grieves and squats on his glass bed.

YELLOW RAPE

Round the ragged city runs the rape.
Rape of the countryside,
yellow rape in place of mellow corn.
Black rape from coal,
from factories born in hope
jagged and wasted now – hope torn.
Rape of the city,
commercial rape, the glitter,
tarnished rusting progression
of Profit's sole obsession.
No living here, no beauty,
except in accidental skyscapes
and in children born to couples raped of pride.

GOOD FRIDAY

On that bad Good Friday
Her arms crept around his neck
And my heart lifted.

They kissed in the Walk
Unaware of my watching
The day everything crumbled.

News came thick and fast
From bad to worse to hopeless
We almost sank without a trace.

But their kissing wrought a smile
Out of my misery.
My smiling brought a kiss
In spite of yours.

Your arms crept around my neck
And my heart lifted
Last Good Friday.

IN DREAMS I WALK THE HILLS AGAIN

In dreams I walk the hills again
With you and dog and friends
I sit on rocks and rest and talk
Then clamber on to reach that view.
What matters if, on waking, the cage waits
If I can stride the hills once more in dreams
And hear the summit's wind toss back our words.

In dreams I swim alone again
And smell the mud and reeds
I fight the flow and work upstream
Then turn and float above the eels.
What matters if, on waking, the cage waits
If I can ride the river in my dreams
Then float among remote reflected clouds.

In dreams I dance with you again
I whirl and dip and sway.
I feel the rhythm's pounding beat
And match my body's twists and leaps.
What matters if, on waking, the cage waits
If I can harness music in my dreams
And feel my brain sing deep within my bones.

BEQUESTS

Gone, all gone now
my ancestors.

Sunk into the dust,
my final destination.

No resting place,
leaving no trace
but a strand of DNA
threading through generations.

No gift from me
wilfully passed on,
no monument, no mark, no smudge.

A smile, a touch, remembered
and bequeathed
to other investors
in good will.

ANTONIO

"Work's good." he said
and leaned upon his hoe,
hands folded, chin on hands.
How many times
had he leaned just so?
Eighty seven years
he still thinks dung
as good as work,
good enough to squeeze
through fingers black with earth.

THE POOL

Staccato shouts of children
Incessant throb of musak
Rasp of passing mopeds
Shrill shout of swifts
        dipping for water.
Whine of a drifting hornet
Droning voices of men in argument
The church bell tolling the hour
Crack of belly-flop on water.

"It is obligatory to shower
before getting into the pool."

PREY

You look happy, hawk, and fat
'Though I hate to think on what
As you wheel about my valley on the trail.

And small birds are very quiet
As you seek your staple diet
For your purpose is to kill and not to fail.

And across the valley, there,
Rising in the crystal air
Is a hotel being built by human hawks.

They will scoop away the pines
Pour hot tarmac on the vines
Shredding silence as they drown the fox's wail.

You look happy, hawks, and fat
'Though I hate to think on what
As you wheel about my valley on the trail.

CAPTAIN

Captain was Persian, of fabulous bloom,
Everyone cooed when he entered a room.
Many cats lived on his elegant street,
But his eyes searched only for Marguerite.

Dreamy and drifting like smoke from the fire,
She never acknowledged his burning desire.
Sinuous and silky she stalked through the night
Presenting to Captain his dream of delight.

Captain oh Captain, I know you are there,
My skin feels the heat of your dangerous stare.
But know that to you I will never succumb
I am waiting for he who is perfect, to come.

MENOPAUSE

MEN – OH PAUSE!
STOP FOR A MOMENT
AND THINK!
WOULDN'T YOU BE GLAD?
YOU WOULD
WOULDN'T YOU
BE
DELIGHTED
OVER THE MOON
DELIRIOUSLY HAPPY?
TO BE RID OF A MONTHLY BLOODY FLUX
THE CURSED CURSE
A REGULAR VISITOR
FOR FORTY YEARS.

STARVING

They're welcome to it
I thought as a child
When I was told
"Eat your meat!
The starving Chinese
Would be glad of it.
Eat it or be shamed
That you do not think of them."

When I tried to keep
Fast in my imagination
That picture,
Millions of them
Starving Chinese
Dissolved into the hungry blur
Which was all my mind could bear.

Could I post it to them?
That hated piece of meat?
Now the face, clearly etched,
Gazed down dumbfounded
By my soggy parcel,
But did not start to eat.

Slyly, yet again,
The meat slid down my dirty dress
Towards the dog.

THE APPLE

Your Apple is never the same as my apple;
Though, in counting, there is one lone apple.
Take it away and we both retain its image
The same?
One or two apples?

I feel it.
With eyes closed I sense its shape,
Make it squeak to my fingers
And prick the stalk into the ball of my thumb.
I stroke the rough remnants of the flower
Then smell the skin warm from my palm
And this is real. This exists, this apple;
And it is not your apple.
Pick it up then
Stroke and touch and feel and smell,
Now it is yours.

THE ARTS CENTRE

Here is an Arts Centre
People make Art
People display Art
People look at Art
As You Like It and Sweeny Todd
Arch Sculpture
Gaudy corner curling posters
Fast fading photographs
Crisp new tickets at the Box-Office
Timetabled lists of helpers
Newly minted sandwiches
Coffee fresh today
All fresh today
Today's Art
    Sculpture
    Theatre
    Painting

We are in the Arts Centre Biz.

PRUNING

And hill to hill they burn the olive branch,
Beacons of peace and faith in next year's crop.
The useless pruned and burned,
Smoke signals rising sign that "All is well."
And voices streaming clear across the gorge
Send boasts and jokes and smug contentment
Where once the flames razed houses
When the olive branch was spurned.

FREE LOVE

"What happened to the love I gave,
the love so freely given?"
"I took it and I made it mine
and then I passed it on."

"But when I gave it thus to you
I gave it to be kept."
"It was not freely given then
if you required a pledge."

"I gave it you, I give it you
such love I can't repress."
"You gave it me, I give it him
there's no more to be said."

CANVASSES

Here am I
A canvas torn
and blown in the wind,
flip flopping my way through life
unable to catch the breeze.

Around me,
sails at full stretch
bear boats of crisp lines
thud thudding their way on course
speeding direct with the wind.

HUNGERFORD

Oh God! That he should run amok in my town,
Shoot my wife where she stood.
And where were you that day,
My God?
My love – gone,
Disappeared in one puff from a madman's maelstrom.
Her body, familiar and responsive,
Filling my hands with delight
Sex in the night
While the children sleep.
Sex and love,
Breakfasts and blarney and bantering,
Past and to come
Taken.
Where were you that day?
Oh Christ!

EL FUERTE

Dusty light on dustier mountain,
Sahara come to Europe.
Sleeping elephant
Sleeping bull-elephant mountain.
Mountain of Moors,
Mountain of massacre.
Then and now are eroded.
The future is rock.

THE MAGGOT

Once there was a girl
Who with one glance
Captured all in the dance
Of her spirit.

Now a maggot mind
In a heaving sweating flesh
Cries
I know your thoughts
I smell your thoughts
They reek of disinterest and boredom.

The maggot mind is hers
not theirs.

I cannot share this
Not with you
Most of all
Not with you
Who would want most
To take it from me
It is unshareable
Especially with you
Who was not born to this.

The maggot is hers
Not theirs
It was there
Long ago
Beneath the dance
Peering through the welcoming glance

You should have run then.

THE HERON

Strutting the reeded water
Stately wader
Attenuated
Snakehead
Wedgehead
Head still
Dead still
A convulsive shimmy into the wind
A judder of concentration
Stillness
Then
Slice
A move so fast it's unseen
Sketched by the brain from water ripples and the fish
    shuddering down the pale stretched neck.

The reed wind shivers as he stalks his dwindling terrain.

THE PRESENT

You took us to a dim and secret place
Where crowded bluebells fill the woods.
The hound stops still, ears cocked, paw raised,
Where the ruined wall sends cobstones to the mud.
The giant bank casts its shadows and we wait
To learn what thing he senses in the gloom,
The raised paw drops.

We'll never know, for he lopes on
To wild garlic clouds by a drunken gate
At a path not taken, 'though he could.
On, on, winding past the turgid pool
To the great stone wall with a space
Wide enough to fit a drawbridge
Through it – the sea!

Oh God! A tiny bay whose tumbled rocks
And gurgling pools are ours alone
For this brief time
As the hound bounds from rock to rock
Then stops to lap fresh water, before it joins the salt.

MOSELEY CHURCH

Have you ever considered the space a church makes
- yard and all –
in the sledgehammer beat
of our noise-ridden lives?
A still small space
in the back and forth, forth and back
circumnavigation of our suburbs.

Whether you think He's there or not,
whether you think He's there at all,
whether you think He is,
someone's belief gave reason
for the crumbling monstrosities,
for the listing gravestones,
for the grey green watery
silent pause of the systems.

For God's sake let us not lose them.

FRIEND YOU MUST TALK

Friend, you must talk,
Must stay more time,
Talk's good for you
As is the wine.

Then timelessness,
The magic goat,
Will repossess
Your attitudes.

You keep yourself
Apart and free,
But cannot leave
Dispassionately.

NOVEMBER

Gloomy
Silver/Smoke
Disappearing
Light.

Soggy
Gold/Brown
Decomposing
Mulch.

Vibrant
Grey/Black
Lacerating
Twigs.

Stillness
Absolute
Threatening
The faintest hint
Of dead cold
To come.

CONCH

Until the living flesh
is hooked from
the deep pink
unseen core of the conch,
the restrained baying melody
cannot be played.

Hook pull and tear
the edible core.
Reach to the convoluted deep,
tug life from its pink sleep.
Goudge the conch
break the shape
pout the lips and play.
Play your victory call.
The exultant baying melody
shouts over all.

CITY PARK

Green water, sludge water,
    City water lake,
    Oval of dirty hope
    Enclosed by sticky trees.
    March wind in June
    Shouts in the branches
Interrupting the ducks
    Who are taking their ease.

    Lone heron, sentinel
    Watcher and seeker
    Waiting his moment
    There in the reeds.
Submariner grebe
    Surfaces and dives
Territorial squirrels
Mouth insults and jibes.

The traffic moans on
Office workers arrive
Peace, a shaky illusion
    In their dusty lives.

QUAKING

QUAKING ACQUIVER WITH QUANTUM DELIGHT
YET QUIET AS A QUAGMIRE AT FRIGHTFUL MIDNIGHT

YOU GASP ON THE GRASS
FITS AND STARTS
POUNDING HEARTS

PULSING HEAVILY
TREMBLING JELLILY

AS SEX TAKES ITS TOLL
OF THE OLD CHOLESTEROL.

OUT OF REACH

My world wanders,
shifts and fades;
dances sometimes,
slightly out of reach,
uncapturable unconquerable
invisible intangible.
The sharp clean focus
of an earlier age
disturbed, disfigured
debilitated, devoured.

His mind wanders,
indistinct;
senile dementia,
totally out of touch,
incapacitated incontinent
uncoordinated uncontrolled.
The concentrated vigour
of his prime of life,
derailed decentralised
disconnected, disappeared.

LOST

I lost me
Somewhere along the way
The 'I' that I was at ten
Disappeared
That boy who dreamed his way
        schemed his way
        screamed his way
Through life love and the playground.

MARGARET

The tea was not drunk
Nor the cup even lifted,
The last cup of tea she made.
Crumbs on the plate,
Perhaps a favourite cake
Or a small sandwich they said;
But the tea not drunk,
Waiting.
Napkin in hand, proving no pain,
She just didn't wake up.
She loved teatime and special things.

RICHES

"I saw you just the other day
I've never seen you look so well."

"Oh yes!" he said
"I've got it sussed,
I've got life by the throat.
Shake it long and hard enough,
it'll yield up its dividends.
That's what I've found.

Oh yes! We're sorted now,
Anne and me.
We've got the lot,
cars, three houses and the yacht.
You name it, I've grabbed it."

And all the while,
the blue schoolboy eyes
fixed, not on me,
but past, to the horizon.

SILENCE

silence drips endlessly in the hidden room
maintaining a frightening status quo
keep the door shut fast
let in no muted boom of traffic
no low voices trailing past

protect the quiet and the space
shut out time blot out thought
cut out schemes
nothing to face
nothing is sought
allow no dreams

LOOKING AT SHAKESPEARE'S TOMB AND THINKING ABOUT POOR YORICK

Here lie the bones that must not be disturbed
And if they were? What could they tell us now?
From childhood we have read and read your words,
Laughed at your jokes and marvelled at your wit.
But where were you?
The real you?
The actor – was that you?
He who played the ghost now truly faded
The sweating strutting player quite quite gone.
The poet, was that you? Great poems like moonlight
Gifted on, but not to us, who grasp at straws of meaning,
Longing for the light. But is that you?
And in the plays we think we find the man
And yes, we find the jokes, the human insight.
But where are you?
And if these bones could talk, what would they tell
Our current writers struggling at the game?
"Keep on! Keep on! And struggle as you must,
But don't seek fame for when at last it comes
It does not come for you
The true you.
All of that is dust.

FOR CONRAD (THE BETJEMAN YEARS)

Now sigh for silent Sundays
Where the lilting Lilac leans
Here, you cannot hear the raindrops
For the rattle of machines.

Now yearn for youth and yesteryear
And river days gone by,
Searching for mushrooms by the weir
We talked there you and I.

Now cry for absent Sundays
And the secret sublime scene
When living, love and leisure
Were the parents of our dreams.

FORTY YEARS ON

You send that look and still
after forty years
my loins dissolve and all the years
dissolve.
Now the passion mounts, then sears.
Ten thousand acts are joined in us
And yet the complex dance, coitus,
repeats no rhythms. It appears
familiar, never is the same
and hot old love still feeds the flame.

SEA CHANGE

For we are going through a sea change, you and I,
No matter what the jokers say
Of menopause, male menopause and all.

We are going through a sea change
And we must see it through.

When all we dreamed or hoped to have
Is in our hands we find,
When days ahead are as countable
As those we've left behind,
Then our pleasant path to nowhere
Is no longer well defined
And comfort's inadmissible
For it drags the clogging mind.

So memories reach further back
Groping for childhood's schemes
And we must help each other
Fulfil those cloudy dreams
For we are going through a sea change, you and I.

THE HARVEST

Stands a bare fig tree
Black against a smoking sunset.
The olive shivers as the first night breeze
Stirs thin smoke columns from the pruners' fires.
And voices ululate from ridge to ridge
In echoing accents of the ancient Moor,
As the last olive sacks are filled, then heaved
By straining mule and labourer to the tracks.

And Luz Lucero shining over all
Peak incandescent in the setting sun,
Below his brilliance – there across the gorge
The ghost village – still there behind the almonds,
Empty since the butchery, the ritual,
The slaughter. Men and women, children,
All.

KILLING

You never hear
The soldier cried
I've told you time and again
That when they shoot
They shoot to kill
And what they kill are men.

You play with board
And manikin
That manikin is me.
But when I shoot
And shoot to kill
You give your sin to me.

You give your sin
To me, my boys,
And then you turn away.
"A brilliant ploy! What strategy!
A job well done."
You say.

You've done the job
More power is gained
The electorate's held in thrall.
But he has killed
And I have killed
And what we've killed, is all.

**Yes, he has sinned
And I have sinned,
We sinned at your behest.
But we are gone
And you are left
How will you now attest?**

POEMS

Sitting in the Job Centre
Filling in forms,
Watching other people
Filling in forms.
Desperation soaks the air,
Desperation, colour of stone.
Faces marked with cold despair
Stress tattooing every bone
Each one a poem, a marked life,
Hammered by circumstance,
Shaped in strife,
Great Poems waiting for their chance.

FAT CAT

Fat cat sitting on the wall
Staring staring staring at us all
You sleek your fur
And you tend your claws
Then stalk inside and raid the stores.

Fat cat weaving through the night
Some acts best completed out of sight
There are those that you kill
There are those that you maim
But they don't matter and they have no name.

Fat cat eat your fish and fat cat drink your milk
Lie down by the fire on the rug made of silk.

THIS ONE

This one girl has been through
the valley of the shadow
of poverty.
This one girl has been choked
at the summit in the clouds
of subjection.
She taught herself
to demean herself.
To say
"Give me give me give me,
I HAVE NOT!
You have done me wrong
so give me."

And they like it,
the manipulators like it.
The manipulators pray
this one girl will drearily stay,
this one girl will querulously say
"Give me!"
For their answer seems an eloquent and logical,
complex and reasonable
"No!"
So manipulators pray
this one girl will never say
"I have,
I have this brain.
I have this body
and I will use

what there is to be used
and reach and seize
and move."

HOUSE OF THE BINNS

Well it's a far cry from the Falklands
Here overlooking the Forth.
The sun for once is beating hot
The gnats and the bees are out.
It's hot as a southern summer
Here in the tangled North.
History's shame and blood and fear
Blended with the living here.

It's odd looking down at the daisies
Whose ancestors grew near
In the long days of treachery
Both there and over here.
While the traffic groaned and the peacocks moaned,
The Belgrano sailed from the battle zone.

THE VILLAGE

Sugar cube houses, roughly packed,
clinging to the terraced slopes.
Thick walled and stout doored,
enclosing their brilliant courtyards.

Crumbling balconies tilt
together for a gossip,
and black eyed windows
stare across the valleys at the sea.

The only space, the Square,
fronted by church, bar and bank.
Religion, sociability and money claiming
the more complex decorative structures.

Linked by a steep stepped alley network,
Each house bedded in the mountain,
guards its secret, intense inner garden.

LOVE POEM TO A GRANDSON

Blood of my blood's blood and bone of my bone's bone
You come into the world now and forever alone.

You relinquished the womb
And at that birthing
Burst in me so great a love
That I can find no words
Except in age-old clichés
So time honoured and time worn
They make emotion sound absurd.

You will go where I may not follow.
You may do things I cannot comprehend.
As you grow older, so do I.
As I am grounded, you will fly.
But this love stays with you, my love
And this love grows with you, my love,
Till we are past my last tomorrow
To the other side of my life's end.

Blood of my blood's blood and bone of my bone's bone,
May you never learn of loneliness, but know to stand alone.

THE BLIZZARD

A million fat white flakes fall thick and fast,
Big as my thumbprint on the window glass.
Now whirling in an upward spiral, now
Drifting sideways caught on trunks and boughs,
Silent and merciless still they come.
Sharp clear outlines where before were none.
The distant view is clarified in white.
Roofs, steeples, statues sharpened to clear sight.
Here, near, the path is blurred, the ground shifts
As the clouding shrouding curtain drifts.

THE VALLEY

The hawk circles high
Checking the valley grid by grid
Moving from H8 to G9
Tension taut from tip to tip.
Barren mountains, indifferent in the singing heat
Hold their separate silent sway.

Below that silence cranks the bus,
Snuffling, grumbling, uncaring beast;
Gorged to the brim with passengers
Drunk from past and present feasts.
Drunk with sight of their azure days,
The Sierra's proud elite.

BACK OFF LIFE

Back off, Life, and let me think.
There's too much going on.
Ten years, the span, will soon be gone
And thinking ends in death.

So little time, so little done,
So much to hear and see and smell
What's gone before, so brief to tell
And telling stops the breath.

Soon enough the prison cell
Unwanted age, the straitened cage
So little strut, so small a stage.
Now let me think and back off, Death.

COMING HOME

In the blue purple of that sky
Hangs the sun, leaden sulky sun.
The red dust stings,
And earth compresses air to sky.

The red river, river of beasts
Pours down the rocks and crams the track.
Crunched down under a sticky tree
Their guardian plays his keening pipes.

A tattered figure walks the dust,
Left footprint deeper than the right.
The stench of blood is with him still
Scorning the goatherd's lifted arm
He tells the man to go with God;
Then takes the track towards his farm,
He takes the track towards his farm.

PRAWNS

Now why do prawns turn pink, My Dear?
Well, here's the reason why.
The reason is, I think, My Dear,
The same for you or I.

They get all hot and bothered, Pet,
It's that does turn them pink.
We, when we're fussed and moithered, Pet,
Turn red as teachers' ink.

We jump into hot water, Love,
Although it makes us cry,
Doing what we didn't oughter, Love,
To reach a higher high.

But when we turn bright pink, My Duck,
We do what prawns do not.
They're forced beyond the brink, My Duck,
We leap into the pot.

THE CHILD

They have the power

They can do with me as they will,
Deny my freedom
Subjucate me to their whim.
I am protected but I have no rights.
I am a child.

BUT

If I scream and shout,
Stamp my foot again, now whine
Now blaze in fury.
Their wills bend to mine,
Affection's conscripts
Co-erced with skill.

Who then has the power?

COSTA BELLOC

Do you remember El Pub,
Amanda?
Do you remember El Pub?
And the joking and the choking
When the ribs got a poking
And the leers and jeers at the Senorita's fears
When a clown's hands strayed a bit too far?
And the boys who breeze and play darts through their knees
Boasting that they cannot understand her?
Do you remember El Pub, Amanda,
Do you remember El Pub?
And the leers and jeers at the Senorita's fears
Who wasn't having any,
Though her charms were not many,
And men paying at the door of the Club?
They read British news
Men who booze
As they cruise
And whose eyes can sidle over girls who idle
With slung boobs in tubes
And their carefully shaved pubes
Drinking poisonous cocktails at the bar?
Do you remember El Pub,
Amanda?
     Do you remember El Pub?

THE 'REAL WORLD'

Sound the bell, yes, sound the bell
    and rally to the mast.
For the old values, the old values
    are disappearing fast.
Victorian vice and cruelty,
Elizabethan lust,
    the Puritans' pride and prurience
    are prisoners of the past.

If we're to make the fastest buck
    we must keep them alive.
We can't allow assumptions
    that the poor are meant to thrive.
So rally every businessman
    who cares about our goals,
    release these virtues of our pasts
    and save our stinking souls.

LOSS

Walking down an ordinary street
In an average town
On a wet summer day -
Glancing sideways –
Momentarily
I see my dead brother
Crossing the road.

Grief attacks in outlandish places
Altering ordinary average faces
Lending the transfigurations
That deepest frustrations
Desire.

CONVERSATION PIECE

"Oh! It's so cold"
"Not 'It is cold', but 'I am cold'"
"You are cold?"
"No, I'm not cold,
But you are cold.
It is not cold."
"But we are told
That it is cold!"
"If you are bold,
You don't feel cold"
"That's what they told
The soldier
Who keeled over
With the cold."

LOST AND FOUND

I lost a lover many years ago.
He brought chocolates and charm
And he took and he trained
And I loved him.
He brought presents and promises
He bonded and restrained
And I desired it.
He brought flattery and flowers
He shackled and he chained
And I was captive.

I lost him and was glad to see him go.

LIFETIMES

There is a lifetime in this room
Incomprehensible to me,
Yet piece by piece
And clue by clue
I absorb their misery.

A dormant canker waiting growth,
Their life's grief soaks through the air.
Its residence,
A bitter hoard,
For centuries fixed there.

And thus and thus and thus and thus,
Waking and sleeping breath,
They beat and beat
Into my brain
Their lifelong, living death.

PARALYSIS

No argument
No exchange of views
No testing of ideas
The words roll around inside my head like peas in a kettledrum.
Rattling and twisting they bounce into an occasional logic.
And how I wish to escape
And how I wish to communicate.
They say I am shut in silence,
If only they could hear the noise inside.

THE GRUB

The little grub eats his way
Around my brain
Through schemes to memory
And back again
He talks
He burrows through me
Like one possessed
He robs me
Of objectivity and zest

SUBURBAN LADY

Suburban lady,
frighteningly sad,
her eyes bulge with memories
of her dead mother. Memories
despoiled.

Suburban lady
clenching her bag,
desperate to lock the mind's cupboard.
"For Jim's sake" she says,
"I must forget this,
forever after
try not to dwell on it.
Jim says to
remember only the happier times,
Mum's laughter."

The old lady was 'In Care',
deliberately gagged and bruised,
battered, tied to her wheelchair
by those whose sympathy was presumed.

Her daughter's terror thoughts persist
in spite of Jim's chiding love.
"But I must learn to accept it
it can't be changed.
Wicked people do exist."

SPILLIKINS

Two heads bent over Spillikins
Both still, both grave,
One dark, one bald,
Absorbed, intent,
Anglo Saxon the man
The child a celt
And at their side the empty mother prattles on.

Outside, the heat of Oxford
Sizzles in the crowded square
An ancient meeting place
Long used for buses,
Heritaged now and bare.
People of Appleton and Fyfield alighted here
Intent on marketing and fun.

Tourists cram the outdoor tables
Resting from the plodding search
Stuffed with History and tea.

Two heads bent over Spillikins.

DOG DAYS

The evening turns towards the chill,
The gnats bite
And the child sobs
Bone tired.
The dog pants on the grass
Old age stretching canine nerves to the limit.
Fingers of cloud sketch
Bars across the western sun
And every creature cries
Thank God!
This day is done.

ENGLISH HEAT WAVE

Dust, crumbling dust,
midge clusters whirring.
Beaten grass hoarding last Spring's juices,
stuck with snap dry twigs.

Spadgers keeping to the shade
lazily poking at rotting vegetation
in the lover green, smother green
of an English Summer.

MICRO MADNESS

He sits before the mesmerising screen,
hands idle, eyes asquint.
The close crammed information
kept distant by his thoughts.

He who'd once rattled with the best of them,
hurling data purposefully
from mind to electronic mind,
now sees hell in small green figures
quivering in their cold ground.

To this end then, the boy's elation led,
the youth's impatience, eating time,
stories of heroes welded to thought's dream.

When did hope curl, then furl the flag,
ambition's white heat cooling to surrender?
Escape now the solitary desire?

The mind's shield fractures as the thoughts unclench.
His eyes blaze at the dwindling screen,
as with a jubilant yell
he pulls the plug.

GUILT

I saw them once
At the top of the tree
Picking apples.
As the car passed
They waved,
Happy.

Last month I passed
By that same narrow road.
They were reaching
Through the barbed wire.
I waved,
Too late.

ON THE COMMON

The rough thrust of the wind in the trees,
The grass pushing upwards like the sea.
Children shout in an earthbound bubble,
Parents plead to go home to tea.

The traffic rasps and aeroplanes hum,
Dogs yelp and yap and greet their friends.
Birds mimic the machine-gun staccato of the child,
Men call as leather ball descends.

Above all, the great grey clouds
Throng the enormous emptiness,
The violent silent vacuum
Which all our dust ingests.

YORKSHIRE SKY

The vast vagrant Yorkshire sky,
endless parabola,
dredging ancient memories of a child's god.

Sea of a sky, mirrored in the moors,
sailed by souls of fortitude.
The wind cries of their love and their terror.

Careering castles casting shadows on the sheep
great sinister slabs of sunken stones
hoarding their histories and their bones.

THE ROSE

It hangs there
the single rose,

Coral scarlet in dark weather,
a beacon beneath the tamarisk tree.

No other rose, just one.

Year on year the dull and dusty bush remains
glowering beneath the tamarisk tree.

We cannot scrap its sulky ugliness,
because next year will come

Its flaming perfect rose.

WHILE YOU CAN

Stare, lovely Senorita, stare.
Hair racing
fluid down the back,
dark eyes,
watchful and absorbed.
Mind ticking,
accepting and rejecting,
on the brink of discovering your own perfection.
Stare, lovely Senorita, stare
in your pre-adolescent
awareness. Learn
what you can. Observe
others and take or leave life
as you wish.
While you can,
stare.

IN LEATHERWORKERS STREET

Elderly men smoulder in Leatherworkers Street
Gazing at the businessman's secretary
Brought for a brief holiday to Crete.

Smoulder as she files a long fingernail
At their table in the fish restaurant,
She poses, he reads the morning's mail.

Over the stones old ladies dressed in black,
Trip gossiping like pigeons, and clutch their matching bags
A lifetime's clutter, safe from attack.

Archaeologists seek ancient treasure trove.
Bones and shards, rubbish dump clues to history,
Lie dark beneath the olive grove.

Work done, her master drops his pen
Which waits with her parings and an old lady's ring
To be found by future History Men.

Present past and future lie at their feet.
Life's miscellany kicked and ignored as
Elderly men smoulder in Leatherworkers Street.

ALMOST DARK

Almost dark, in the park at sunset
the empty roundabout turns and turns.
The woman watches;
    her memory burns.
Where is the shrieking child
in love with speed,
hair lifting, floating wild?
The trees and lake recede
into a dancing blur.
Where is the child?
The woman watches;
    the roundabout turns.
She remembers, he climbed on.
She remembers, he stopped it,
    before he savaged her.
The child is gone.
Here is the woman.
Here is the shrivelled shell
that held so sweet a nut.
Where is the child?

MODEL

Flesh, soft elastic and warm,
clothes the miraculously
jointed skeleton.

The curve of the spine,
fragile and delicate,
echoes the vulnerability
of the mouth,

negating the
hard fought for
toughly won,
worldly wise
cynicism
of the eyes.

AFFLUENCE

LABEL US AND FORGET US
THE 'AFFLUENT SOUTH EAST'.
LOSE IN YOUR EMPTY DEFINITIONS
THE CHILDREN WHO CANNOT SPEAK,
OLD LADIES FREEZING IN KENT WINTERS.
THE YOUTH WHO LIVE IN DIRT AND SHAME.

CHAMPIONS OF THE RICH WHOEVER THEY MAY BE
CHAMPIONS OF 'THE HARD WORKING FAMILY'
PLATITUDINISING
EMPTILY
MOUTHING YOUR SOLUTIONS,

FORGET
THAT CHEEK BY JOWL WITH AFFLUENCE
LIVE
THE POOR.

ANDALUCIAN HAIKU

Almond braseras
toast feet under round tables
as we watch T.V.

The bulldozer growls
impatiently awaiting
the passing of goats.

Mickey Mouse Tee Shirts
teetering on stillettos
avoiding mule dung.

SUMMER FRIENDS

Dream days, Goodbye days,
Swanning slowly by days,
Hug you look you in the eye days,
God it's been good
That's understood.
See you one day
We'll come and stay;
Maybe and perhaps
Avoiding the traps
That friendships imply.
Friends swanning by,
Slowly floating, Goodbye.

Made in the USA
Charleston, SC
15 October 2015